An Amish Quilt
in a Day

— Variations of Roman Stripe

By Eleanor Burns

To Amy — My Niece

A Pennsylvania Sweetheart

Illustrations by Patricia Knoechel
Cover Photography by David Steutel
Inside Cover Photography by David Steutel and Brian Steutel

Typesetting by Headline
Layout by David Steutel

First Printing — April, 1986

ISBN 0-922705-05-4

Quilt in a Day®
1955 Diamond Street, Unit A
San Marcos, CA 92069
(619) 436-8936

Table of Contents

Sewing Instructions for the Overlock are included.

Introduction

Warm summer Sunday afternoons were always special to me in the late 1960's. We'd take a break from our graduate studies at Pennsylvania State University and drive around the beautiful countryside surrounding State College, hoping to come upon a horse drawn buggy traveling slowly down the road. Perhaps we'd catch a glimpse of an Amish family on their way to a Sunday gathering, with their beautiful children shyly peaking out the back window. The air was never fresher as we drove past well-kept farms alive with beautiful flower beds and manicured gardens.

As I rush through life, there are moments I reflect upon their simple, austere life. Although their lifestyle and manner of dress is "plain," their quilts show great freedom and bright splashes of color.

It was during the third week of December, 1985, that I made my first Roman Stripe quilt on the overlock sewing machine. The quilt was for my special teenage niece, Amy. Black is a favorite color of hers, along with purples, blues, and pinks. The Amish quilt seemed perfect! Hers was the fifth quilt I made that week, with Good St. Nick breathing down my neck!

Just as the Amish see their children as a gift from God, I feel a special joy for Amy. All I thought of was how that bright quilt would keep her warm during the Pennsylvania winter. I certainly didn't use the same methods as the Amish while cutting or sewing Amy's quilt as I zipped through the process, but my feelings toward the quilt as an extension of love were the same.

With the use of the five thread overlock, rotary cutter, and 6" x 24" ruler with 45° line, I had the top pieced and ready to tie in a short five hours, all with straight sewing. Of course, you can use a conventional sewing machine and also hand quilt the top if so desired.

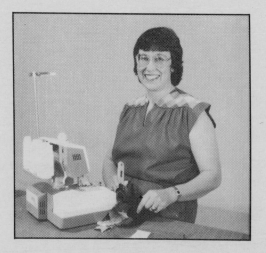

Quilts have been used in abundance to add a decorative accent and warmth to "country homes." Because of its simplicity in design and the solid colors, this particular Amish quilt fits beautifully into "modern homes" when done in the popular mauves, greys, pinks, purples, and turquoises.

Color Selection

Choosing colors for the Amish Quilt is exciting because regardless of what is choosen, the black intensifies and dramatizes all colors.

Look at the color photos and decide how you want your quilt to look: monochromatic (all shades of one color) or with contrasting value (mixture of light, medium, and dark.)

Part A: The striped part of the block, Part A, is made up of **5 solid colors.** These may be the same 5, or the same 10 throughout, or may be a random mixture of many solid colors. The Amish generally select from red to green on the color wheel: brightly colored blues, greens, purples, and reds. The one color they use sparingly is yellow.

If you choose to use the same 5 colors throughout, two will dominate in the finished quilt because of the reversal in the sewing and cutting procedure. If you use 10 different colors consistently, 4 will dominate in the finished quilt.

While you are selecting your colors, stack the fabric bolts on top of each other so you see just a small amount of fabric showing. Stand back and squint to see their relationship to each other. Consider these suggestions:

Monochromatic Gradation — Take a color or hue and choose 5 different values of that color and arrange them in a light to dark order. This monochromatic blending gives a soft look.

Examine the blue and purple quilt layouts to see how two monochromatic groups of color were used. The quilt features 10 different colors, with 4 dominating.

Analogous Colors — Use colors side by side on the color wheel as red, red violet, violet, and blue violet.

Contrasting Value — Mix light, medium, and dark colors as the "crayon box" colors of the rainbow: violet, blue, green, orange, and red for a strong effect. Pastel colors of the rainbow as soft lavendar and blue, mint green, apricot, and pink create a totally different effect.

Calicos – Even though this book was written with reproducing the look of the Amish quilts in mind, one has to realize that solids and dark colors are not in every quiltmakers interest. Since this sewing method is so simple, all should try it. Consider a totally different look utilizing some or all calicos in Part A.

Four Solids and One Print or Stripe: Arrange the colors so the print or stripe falls in the center of Part A, or color 3. For example, choose a print or stripe with both pink and green in it. Make colors 1 and 2 two shades of solid pink, and colors 4 and 5 two shades of solid green. When the blocks are set together, pink will dominate in one block, and green will dominate in the other.

Exact yardage is given for using just 5 colors in the baby quilt and wallhangings. For the larger quilts, yardage is given for using either five or ten different colors. If you choose to use many colors, total up the yardage for the five colors, divide by the number of colors you are using, and purchase that much yardage for each color.

Part B: The other side of the block, Part B, is traditionally **solid black.** However, other color choices that have been used effectively include brown, navy, slate grey, and mauve. You may choose to use the same color throughout, or a mixture of these colors.

Borders: Narrow borders surround the blocks in the same colors as in Part A. For a bright finish, instructions for a narrow striped band using all leftover pieces is included.

Backing: In this Amish quilt, the backing is brought from the back around to the front and becomes the last border. Therefore, the backing should be the same color as Part B in the block.

Sample Paste Up Sheet

    With a glue stick, paste up small swatches of fabric to
visualize how your blocks will look. The swatches can be removed
and changed with a glue stick.
    Do two separate paste-ups if you are working with 10
consistent colors.

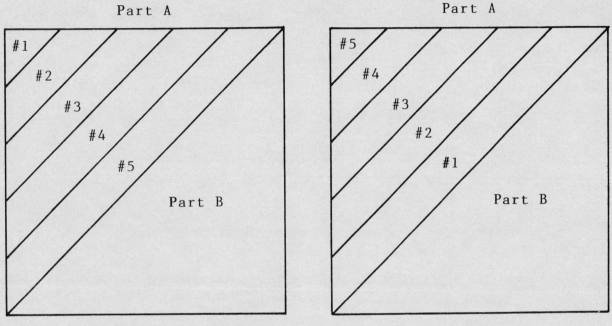

#1 and #5 will dominate in the finished quilt if you sew the same
five colors together consistently.

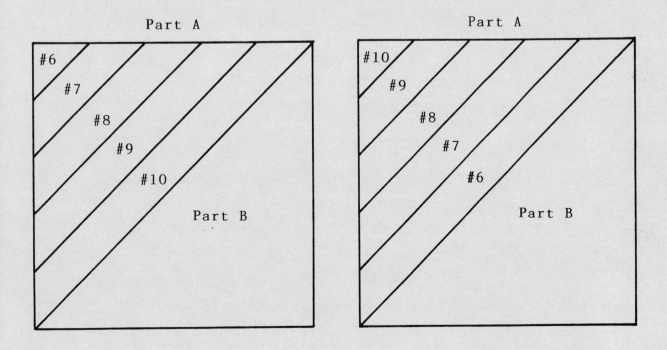

Fabric Selection

Fabric: Select a good quality of 100% cotton 45" wide for your blocks and backing. Prewash the light and dark fabrics separately with soap in a gentle wash cycle. Dark colors as red, burgundy, navy, rust, and brown may bleed. When you prewash these colors, set them by adding salt to the wash water.

Batting: Select bonded polyester batting for the inside of your quilt in your choice of thicknesses. Keep in mind that the thick battings as 8 oz. or 10 oz. show the most dimension when tied and are the warmest. You may want a thin batting, 2 - 3 oz., for a wallhanging or for hand quilting your finished top.

Floss: Use all strands of embroidery floss, crochet thread, pearl cotton, candlewicking yarn, or 100% wool yarn for tying down the blocks.

Supplies

Thread: Choose a large spool of a neutral shade of polyester spun thread for your blocks and a second large spool the same shade as Part B in your blocks.

Cutting Tools: For quick and accurate measuring and cutting, use a rotary cutter, a thick 6" x 24" see-thru ruler with a bias line marked on it, and a special board for cutting on with a rotary cutter.

Pins: Use extra-long, 1 3/4" sharp pins with the colored heads for pinning and a curved upholstery needle for tying.

Presser Foot: Use a general purpose presser foot as illustrated. Use the edge of the foot as a guide for a generous 1/4" seam allowance. Do not use a foot that results in a skimpy seam allowance.

Presser Foot

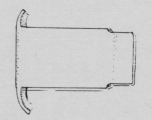

Magnetic Seam Guide

Magnetic Seam Guide: A magnetic seam guide helps when stitching accurate, straight seam allowances.

Walking Foot: An even feed foot, or walking foot, is an optional but useful aid to use while sewing the blocks and borders in this quilt. With the walking foot, two layers of fabric move together while being sewn and do not shift and become distorted.

Yardage Charts

16 Block Wallhanging or Baby Quilt

BLOCKS: 16 or 20		BORDER
Part A: 1/3 yd. each of 5 different colors Part B: 3/4 yd.	Plus	1/3 yd. of one color
Backing (Same as Part B)		1 1/2 yds.
Batting		38" x 46" or 1 1/2 yds.
Approximate Finished Size		35" x 43"

24 Block Wallhanging

BLOCKS: 24		BORDER
Part A: 1/3 yd. each of 5 different colors Part B: 1 1/3 yds.	Plus	1/2 yd. of one color
Backing (Same as Part B)		2 yds.
Batting		38" x 54" or 2 yds.
Approximate Finished Size		35" x 51"

Lap Quilt

BLOCKS: 48		BORDER
Part A: 3/4 yd. each of 5 different colors or 1/3 yd. of 10 Part B: 2 yds.	Plus	7/8 yd. of one color
Backing (Same as Part B)		4 1/2 yds.
Batting		65" x 80" or 4 1/2 yds.
Approximate Finished Size		62" x 77"

Twin Quilt

BLOCKS: 60		Coverlet	BORDER	Bedspread
Part A: 3/4 yd. each of 5 different colors or 3/8 yd. each of 10 Part B: 3 yds.	Plus	1 yd. of one color	or	1 yd. of one color 1 5/8 yds. of one color
Backing (Same as Part B)		6 1/2 yds.		7 yds.
Batting		65" x 95" or 6 1/2 yds.		77" x 107" or 7 yds.
Approximate Finished Size		61" x 91"		73" x 104"

Double Quilt

BLOCKS: 80		Coverlet	BORDER	Bedspread
Part A: 1 yd. each of 5 different colors or 1/2 yd. each of 10 Part B: 4 yds.	Plus	1 1/8 yds. of one color	or	1 1/8 yds. of one color 1 3/4 yds. of one color
Backing (Same as Part B)		6 1/2 yds.		10 yds.
Batting		80" x 95" or 6 1/2 yds.		92" x 107" or 10 yds.
Approximate Finished Size		76" x 91"		88" x 103"

Queen Quilt

BLOCKS: 100		BORDER		
		Coverlet		Bedspread
Part A: 1 1/4 yds. each of 5 different colors or 5/8 yd. each of 10 Part B: 5 yds.	Plus	1 1/3 yds. of one color	or	1 1/3 yds. of one color 2 yds. of one color
Backing (Same as Part B)		10 yds.		10 yds.
Batting		95" x 95" or 10 yds.		107" x 107" or 10 yds.
Approximate Finished Size		91" x 91"		104" x 104"

King Quilt

BLOCKS: 144		BORDER		
		Coverlet		Bedspread
Part A: 1 5/8 yds. each of 5 different colors or 7/8 yd. each of 10 Part B: 7 yds.	Plus	1 1/2 yds. of one color	or	1 1/2 yds. of one color 2 1/3 yds. of one color
Backing (Same as Part B)		10 yds.		11 1/4 yds.
Batting		110" x 110" or 10 yds.		122" x 122" or 11 1/4 yds.
Approximate Finished Size		106" x 106"		118" x 118"

Tearing or Cutting Charts

Choose either cutting or tearing your strips according to your preference, but use the same method for all strips. Each method has its advantages and disadvantages! When tearing your strips, you have the perfect straight of the grain, but must tolerate the never ending dangling strings and ironing. You avoid pulled edges, strings and ironing when cutting your strips, but it is also very difficult to keep the strips on the straight of the grain. In fact, if you are not careful while cutting, your strips may take on a "V" shape rather than a "straight" shape.

Which ever method you choose, follow the Tearing or Cutting Charts on pages 12 and 13 for the number of strips for each color and number and widths of the borders.

The pieces for Part B are cut or torn after Part A is sewn and measured.

Tearing Your Strips

If the fabric has been cut from the bolt, put the fabric on the straight of the grain. Cut a 1/2" nick into the selvage edge about 1" from the edge. Tear from one selvage to the other. If you don't get a straight edge, nick and tear again until you do.

Nick and tear accurate 1 3/4" strips for the blocks and wide strips for the borders from selvage to selvage following the cutting and tearing charts. Torn strips must be pressed before sewing.

When sewing torn strips, measure the 1/4" seam allowance from the first true thread rather than from the "fuzzy" edge.

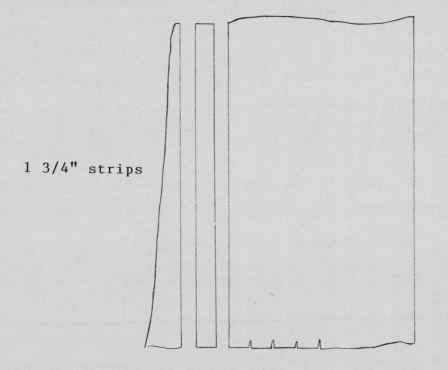

1 3/4" strips

Cutting Your Strips

If any fabric is not easy to tear, and is getting pulled threads and ragged edges, it should be cut into strips. The quickest, most accurate method of doing this is with a large rotary cutter, a thick gridded, see-thru 6" x 24" ruler, and a cutting board.

Tear your fabric to put it on the straight of the grain. Fold the fabric in fourths, matching up the torn straight edge. It is sometimes impossible to match up the selvage sides!

Lay your fabric on the board with most of it laying off to the right. Place the see-thru ruler on the very edge of the fabric on the left.

With your left hand, firmly hold the ruler with 4 fingers. Keep the little finger on the mat to hold the ruler steady.

With the rotary cutter in your right hand, begin cutting with the blade off the fabric on the mat. Put all of your strength into the rotary cutter as you cut away from you and trim off the torn ragged edge.

Move your ruler over every 1 3/4", measuring and cutting carefully and accurately.

Check every few strips to make certain that they are straight. If you are getting crooked strips, tear to put the fabric back on the straight of the grain, refold, and resume your cutting.

If you are left-handed, reverse the cutting process with the fabric on the left and the ruler on the right.

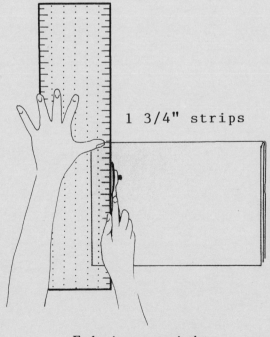

1 3/4" strips

Fabric on right
Ruler on left

16 Block Wallhanging or Baby Quilt

BLOCKS: 16 or 20	BORDERS
Part A: (4)-1 3/4" of each color for 5	(4)-2 1/2"

24 Block Wallhanging

BLOCKS: 24	BORDERS
Part A: (5)-1 3/4" of each color for 5	(6)-2 1/2"

Lap Quilt

BLOCKS: 48	BORDERS
Part A: (10)-1 3/4" of each color for 5 (5)-1 3/4" of each color for 10	(6)-4 1/2"

Twin Quilt

BLOCKS: 60	BORDERS Coverlet	Bedspread
Part A: (12)-1 3/4" of each color for 5 (6)-1 3/4" of each color for 10	(7)-4 1/2"	(7)-4 1/2" (8)-6 1/2"

Double Quilt

BLOCKS: 80	BORDERS	
	Coverlet	Bedspread
Part A: (16)-1 3/4" of each color for 5 (8)-1 3/4" of each color for 10	(8)-4 1/2"	(8)-4 1/2" (8)-6 1/2"

Queen Quilt

BLOCKS: 100	BORDERS	
	Coverlet	Bedspread
Part A: (20)-1 3/4" of each color for 5 (10)-1 3/4" of each color for 10	(9)-4 1/2"	(9)-4 1/2" (10)-6 1/2"

King Quilt

BLOCKS: 144	BORDERS	
	Coverlet	Bedspread
Part A: (29)-1 3/4" of each color for 5 (15)-1 3/4" of each color for 10	(11)-4 1/2"	(11)-4 1/2" (12)-6 1/2"

Examples of Finished Block 1 and Block 2

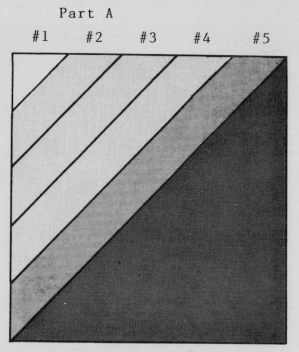

Part A

#1 #2 #3 #4 #5

Part B

Block 1

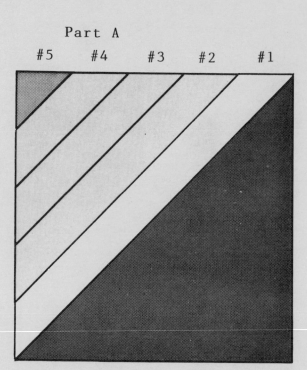

Part A

#5 #4 #3 #2 #1

Part B

Block 2

Machine Settings

1/4" Seam Allowance

Check to see if using the edge of your presser foot as a guide gives you a 1/4" seam allowance. A generous 1/4" is preferred to a skimpy one. If using your presser foot as a guide produces a skimpy seam, consider using a magnetic seam guide.

Some machines have the needle off-center to the left, and consequently a wide seam is produced when the edge of the presser foot is used as a guide. Experiment to find the proper adjustment to get that 1/4" seam.

15 Stitches Per Inch

If your sewing machine does not list stitches per inch, but lists numbers from 1 to 4, set the stitch length at 2. It is not necessary to backstitch at the beginning and end of each strip.

Sewing the Blocks

Making Part A

Arrange the strips for sewing. If you are using just 5 colors, and wish to sew them together consistently in the same order so that colors #1 and #5 dominate, arrange them in this order:

Repeat with the second set of 5 colors if you are using 10 different colors.

If you are using a mixture of colors for a random look, stack up the strips in five equal piles.

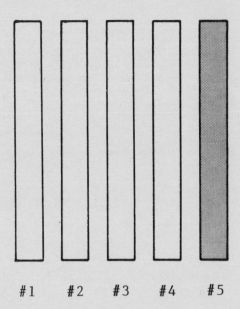

#1   #2   #3   #4   #5

Place Strip #2 right sides together to Strip #1, with Strip #1 on the bottom.

Seam the strips together lengthwise with a consistent 1/4" seam allowance and 15 stitches per inch.

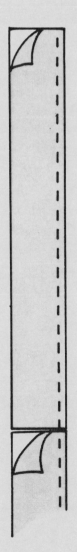

As soon as you finish stitching one strip of #2 right sides together to #1, butt on a second set of strips behind the first and continue stitching in the same manner.

Stitch together all #1 and #2 strips.

Open up the #1/#2 strip.

Place #3 strip right sides together to #2.

Seam the strips together lengthwise in the same manner.

Use accuracy in your stitching.

1/4" Seam Allowance

15 Stitches Per Inch

If one color is particularly long, and that strip makes it difficult to butt on the next section, trim it even with the other colors before butting on the new strip.

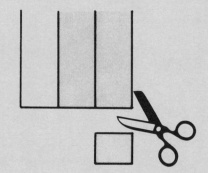

Continue adding on strips #4 and #5 until each section is made up of all 5 colors approximately 45" long.

Cut the threads holding the units together.

You should have a total of this many Part A's.

Quilt Size	# of Part A's
Wallhanging (16)	3 1/2
Baby Quilt	4
Wallhanging (24)	5
Lap Robe	10
Twin Quilt	12
Double Quilt	16
Queen Quilt	20
King Quilt	29

Press all seams to one side. Press on both the right side and the wrong side of Part A. Make certain that no part of the strips have been folded over.

Overlock Instructions

The sewing instructions are identical. Use accuracy and consistency in your seam allowance.

Making Part B

From the wrong side, measure the width of the finished and pressed Part A, or the sewn together strips. Measure from one outside raw edge to the other in several different places to find an average number.

Measurement _____".

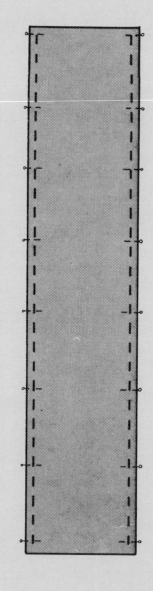

With the Part B fabric, cut or tear that measurement selvage to selvage. Make as many Part B's as you have Part A's.

Quilt Size	# of Part B's
Wallhanging (16)	3 1/2
Baby Quilt	4
Wallhanging (24)	5
Lap Robe	10
Twin Quilt	12
Double Quilt	16
Queen Quilt	20
King Quilt	30

Place a Part A and Part B right sides together.

Pin together every 5". Smooth and stretch apart either piece as you pin so the outside edges of both pieces meet.

Sew on the long striped sides of both edges with a 1/4" seam allowance and 15 stitches per inch.

Sew from pin to pin so the pieces do not stretch and distort. If necessary, use an even feed or walking foot to sew these sections without stretching.

Sew together all Part A's and Part B's in this manner.

Overlock Instructions

Read all basic instructions for making Part B on page 18, and make these adjustments in your pinning.

Pin the strips together 1" in from the edges to avoid hitting the overlock's knife with the pins when stitching.

If any fragments of Part A stick out along the edges from under Part B, use the raw edge of Part B as your guide and trim away the fragments as you sew.

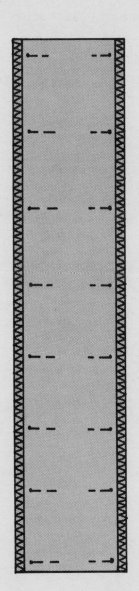

Cutting the Blocks

Lay out one sewn together A/B strip on the special cutting mat.

Lay a second strip on top with the colors reversed from the first.

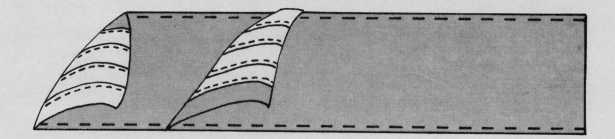

Reverse or alternate the order between the two strips so that when you cut, you have an even number of Block 1's and Block 2's when you are finished.

Bias Line or
45° line on
6" x 24" ruler

Place the bias line or 45° line of the 6" x 24" ruler on the straight top edge of the A/B strip. Place the edge of the ruler in the corner of the right side of the A/B strip.

Cut along the edge of the ruler with the rotary cutter.

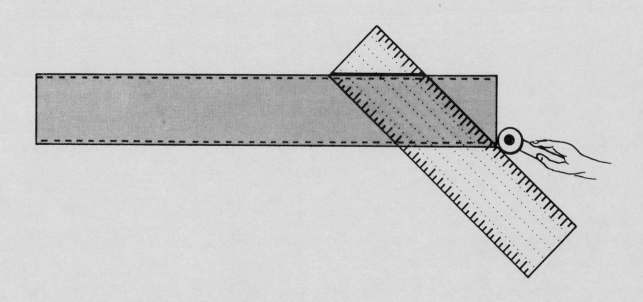

Flip the ruler over. Match the bias line with the top straight edge and the tip of the strip where the last block was cut. Cut again.

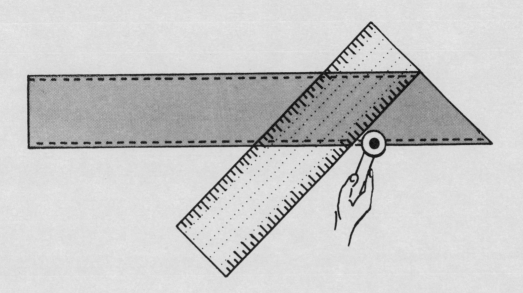

Continue across the strips flipping the ruler over, matching the bias line with the straight edge and the tip, and cutting.

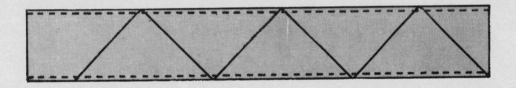

Overlock Instructions
Follow the basic instructions. The stitches across the tips can easily be removed by dropping the rotary cutter blade against them.

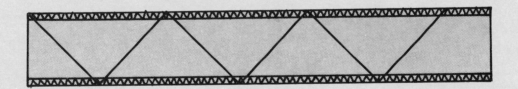

All sewers can get 5 blocks per strip. However, some can get 6 blocks due to the width of their fabric. Cut 2 strips to see if you get 10 or 12. If you get 12, do some figuring: divide 6 into the total number of blocks you need to get the number of strips to cut. Any remaining strips may be cut up for a colorful band in the borders.

Make as many blocks as you need for your quilt.

Size Quilt	# of Blocks
Wallhanging (16)	16
Baby	20
Wallhanging (24)	24
Lap	48
Twin	60
Double	80
Queen	100
King	144

Tear the threads out of the tips of your blocks by separating the two pieces apart and tugging gently at the seams.

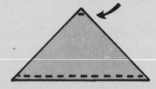

Press the seams to the dark side. Snip the tips from the corners of the blocks.

If you used 5 colors consistently, separate the blocks into two separate piles for Block 1's and Block 2's.

If you used 10 different colors, separate them into 4 piles.

Laying Out the Pattern

A unique feature of this quilt is that there are many different ways to arrange the blocks. The different designs have been graded as to the skill level one needs when setting the blocks together based on if there are stripes to match or not. If you do not care to match the stripes exactly, any of the patterns would be suitable for you.

Elementary Skill Level

Blocks set together in this traditional fashion are easy to sew together because there are no stripes to match. However, one must be careful not to stretch the black, or Part B, while sewing the blocks together as this piece has been cut on the bias.

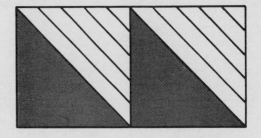

Intermediate Skill Level

Blocks set together in this fashion are a bit more difficult because of the stripes to match, but still fairly easy. The easiest way to match these is to look and line up the stripes, "finger pin" or squeeze them together tightly with your fingers, and then sew over them.

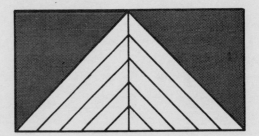

Advanced Skill Level

This is the most difficult arrangement of blocks to set together so the stripes run even from one block to the next. If you are creatively designing your own, avoid this arrangement or choose to not match them perfectly.

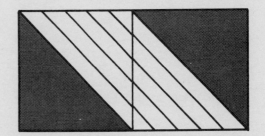

Experiment with different designs following the charts and photographs before choosing one of the pattern layouts! Arrange the blocks accordingly following the dimensions as listed below. Repeat the patterns to get the quilt size you need.

To identify the various patterns easily, names have been given to each of the designs to be used with this book only.

You can be simple and traditional in your design as in the Roman Stripe, or be creative in your design, as framing the Diamond pattern with Flying Geese in a large quilt layout. You could eliminate the top and bottom rows of the twenty-four block wallhangings for a sixteen block wallhanging, or use them as the center of your quilt, and build upon them.

If you have made four separate piles of Block 1's and Block 2's by using 10 different colors, plan your design carefully to utilize equal numbers of all 4 blocks.

The numbered side of the block designates the striped side.

Quilt	Across	Down
Wallhanging - 16 Blocks	4 Blocks	4 Blocks
Baby Quilt - 20 Blocks	4 Blocks	5 Blocks
Wallhanging - 24	4 Blocks	6 Blocks
Lap Robe - 48 Blocks	6 Blocks	8 Blocks
Twin Quilt - 60 Blocks	6 Blocks	10 Blocks
Double Quilt - 80 Blocks	8 Blocks	10 Blocks
Queen Quilt - 100 Blocks	10 Blocks	10 Blocks
King Quilt - 144 Blocks	12 Blocks	12 Blocks

Overlock Instructions

These pattern layouts are based on sewing the blocks with a 1/4" seam allowance, and ending up with an approximate 7" to 7 1/2" square finished block. Based on the amount of fabric actually trimmed off by the overlock, the overall size of the finished blocks may be larger. You may not need as many blocks for your particular size quilt.

Roman Stripe - Elementary Skill Level

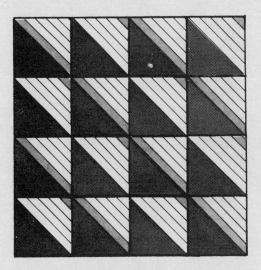
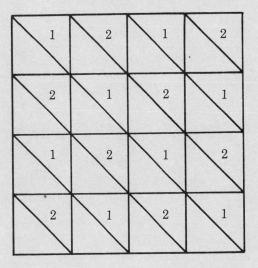

Diamond - Intermediate Skill Level

Variation
of
Diamond

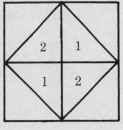

Flying Geese - Intermediate Skill Level

For an interesting pattern, combine the Flying Geese and the Diamond design.

Windmill - Elementary Skill Level

 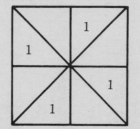

Work the Windmill design in groups of 4. Experiment by mixing the Diamond and Windmill.

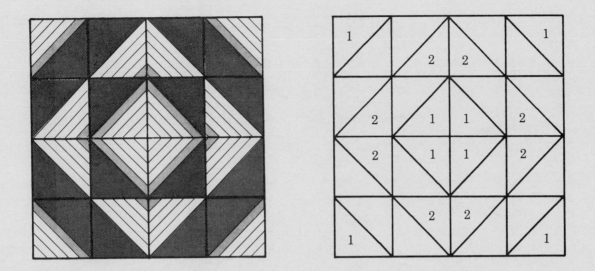

You can use this as the center of a large quilt. Lay this out and build the blocks from the center out.

Twenty-four Block Wallhanging — Intermediate Skill Level

You can also reproduce this design for a sixteen block wall hanging by removing the top and bottom rows.

Sewing the Blocks Together

Lay the blocks out in order following your particular quilt size.

Flip the second vertical row right sides together onto the first vertical row.

Pick up the pairs of blocks in the first vertical row from the bottom to the top. The pair at the top will be on the top of the stack.

Stack up each one of the vertical rows from the bottom to the top, having the top block on the top of the stack each time.

Write the row number on a small piece of paper and pin it through all thicknesses of fabric.

Example Illustration: Your quilt may have a different number of rows.

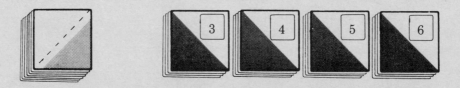

Start in the upper left hand corner. Pick up blocks #1 and #2.

Stitch down about 1/2" to anchor the two together. Match and fingerpin by squeezing tightly the first stripe to match. Stitch. Match and fingerpin the next stripe. Stitch.

If there are no stipes to match as in the Roman Stripe, fingerpin the other corner of the block and ease the two to meet. Stitch.

Do not cut the threads or lift the presser foot.

Pick up blocks #3 and #4. Butt them right behind the first two.

Anchor the two with 1/2" of stitching. Fingerpin the stripes or corners as before. Ease the two to meet. Stitch.

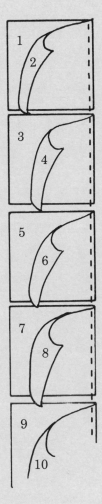

Continue butting on #5 and #6 in the same manner.

Butt and stitch all the blocks until the two rows are completed.

Do not cut the blocks apart.

Overlock Instructions

It is difficult to match and butt on the blocks closely behind each other while using the overlock. Butt as closely as you can, and utilize this "chain stitching" to keep the blocks in order.

Some overlock sewers have choosen not to use the overlock in this step because they were not able to get perfect matches in stripes.

Place the block at the top of the third vertical row right sides together to #2.

Ease and stitch the two to meet, matching all stripes and corners.

Butt, ease, and stitch the second block in the third vertical row onto #4

Butt, ease, and stitch the third block in the third vertical row onto #6.

Continue sewing all blocks in all vertical rows in the same manner.

Do not clip the threads holding the blocks together.

Example Illustration: Yours may look different according to the size of quilt.

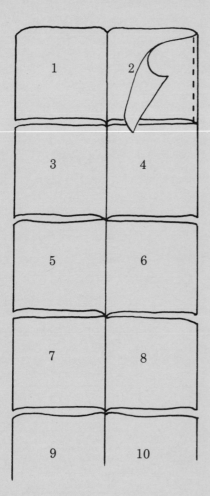

Flip the top row down onto the second row with right sides together.

Match, ease, and stitch the stripes and blocks to meet. Where the two blocks are joined by a thread, match the seam carefully. Push one seam allowance up on one side, and one down on the other side.

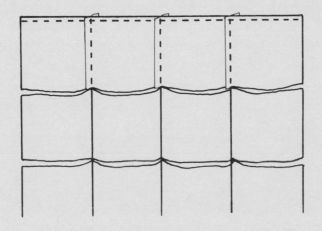

Stitch all horizontal rows in the same manner.

Staystitch all around the outside edge of your quilt with 1/8" seam allowance and 15 stitches per inch. This is to prevent stretching and distortion on the pieces cut on the bias, and must be done before the borders are added.

Sewing the Borders and Backing

Piecing the Borders

Follow the individual Cutting or Tearing Charts for the widths of each border cut or torn from selvage to selvage. Seam the strips of each color into long pieces by flashfeeding.

Lay the first strip right side up. Lay the second strip right sides to it.

Backstitch, stitch the short ends together, and backstitch again.

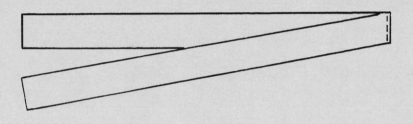

Take the strip on the top and fold it so the right side is up.

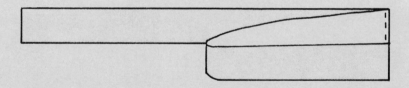

Place the third strip right sides to it, backstitch, stitch, and backstitch again.

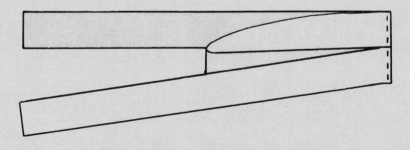

Continue flashfeeding all the short ends together into long pieces for each color.

Clip the threads holding the strips together.

Piecing the Colorful Narrow Striped Band

This is an optional band of color you may choose to make with all of your left-over ends from your blocks.

Cut any remaining pieces into 2" sections. Trim off any diagonal ends.

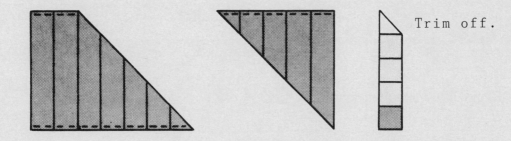

Trim off.

If you choose to use any sections of the Part B color, the colorful band will become long quickly. Using any size pieces does not detract from the beauty of this band. However, the choice is yours, to make it consistent in color and size, or random in color and size.

Flashfeed the small sections into larger sections by placing two small sections right sides together, stitching, and butting on two new sections.

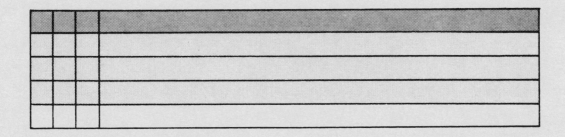

Using the same sewing method as just described in sewing the long border strips together, sew the larger sections of the colorful band into one long piece.

If the colorful band is not quite long enough to go the whole way around the quilt, piece together any leftover strips and cut them into 2" sections.

Sew this colorful band on later after the first border has been added to the quilt top.

Piecing the Backing Fabric

The backing may need to be pieced to get the desired length and width for the backing on the quilt.

Equally fold and cut the backing fabric into these sections:

Quilt Size	Number of Sections
16 Block Wallhanging	1
Baby Quilt	1
24 Block Wallhanging	1
Lap Robe	2
Twin Quilt	2
Double Coverlet	2
Double Bedspread	3
Queen Quilt	3
King Quilt	3

Seam the selvage edges of the pieces together lengthwise using the same color of thread and a 1/2" seam allowance.

If you are going to embroider your name and date on the back of your quilt, the backing fabric will now fit easily into an embroidery hoop. Consider adding your state also as many quilts end up traveling about the country.

Piecing the Batting

The batting may need to be pieced to get the desired size. Cut and butt the two edges closely together without overlapping.

Whipstitch the edges together with a double strand of thread. Do not pull the threads tightly as this will create a hard ridge visible on the outside of the quilt.

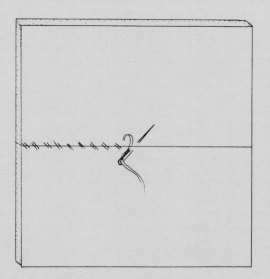

Finishing the Quilt

Measure the long sides of the quilt and cut two border pieces that length. Lay your borders out on a table with the right side up.

Place the edge of the quilt right sides to the borders. Make certain that the pieces are laying flat and not stretched.

Pin and sew the borders on and fold the borders out flat.

Measure and cut borders for the two short sides. Pin and sew the borders to the two short sides and fold them out flat.

If you are adding on a colorful striped band and/or a second border, add them in the same manner.

Fit the Quilt to the Bed

Before adding the backing, lay the quilt out on the bed to check the fit. Get an idea of how much black or Part B should show around the outside edge to get the proper fit. Keep in mind that the quilt will "shrink" approximately 4" in the length and width after completion of tying and "stitching in the ditch."

Adding the Backing Fabric

Lay the quilt top on the backing fabric. Corner it.

Find the shortest measurement in either the length from the quilt top to the outside edge of the backing fabric, or the width from the quilt side to the outside edge of the backing fabric. Trim the two sides to equal that measurement.

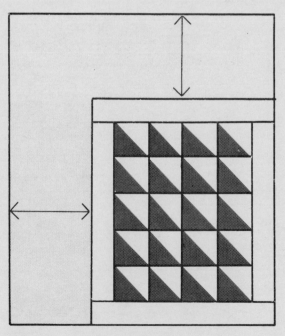

For Example: For a 4" edge of backing fabric showing on the right side of the quilt, add 16" to both the length and width when cutting the backing fabric.

For a 6" edge of backing fabric showing on the right side of the quilt, add 24" to both the length and width when cutting the backing fabric.

Separate the quilt top and the quilt backing.

Fold all 4 sides of the quilt in half and mark with pins.

Fold all 4 sides of the backing in half and mark with pins.

With the quilt and backing right sides together, match the center pins on one side. Stitch from the center out to within 3/8" from the edge.

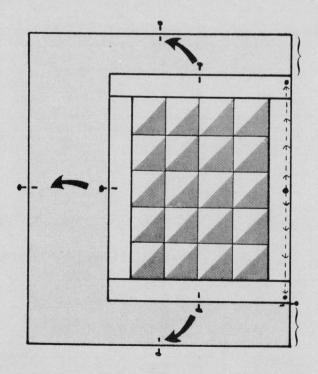

Measure the distance from the outside edge of the quilt to the outside edge of the backing.

Place a pin on the opposite side equal to that measurement.

Stretch or ease the remaining half of the quilt top to the backing within that measurement.

Go to the opposite side and repeat this step, maintaining the same measurements.

Sew the third side in the same manner.

Repeat this step on the fourth side, leaving a 2' opening in the middle of the side.

Arrange the quilt so the backing fabric evenly frames the quilt top.

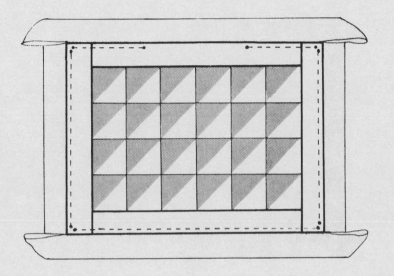

Press the excess backing fabric in the corners to one side.

Following the fold line just pressed in, stitch from the border to the corner, ending 1/2" from the outside edge. This forms a mitered corner once the quilt is turned right side out.

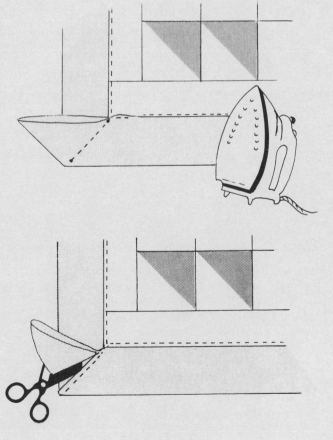

Trim the excess fabric from the corner once the stitching is completed.

Lay the quilt on top of the batting.

With the wrong side of the quilt out, smooth and arrange the quilt so the backing fabric evenly frames the quilt top.

Cut the batting the same size as the top. **Be extremely** careful not to cut into the quilt while trimming the batting away.

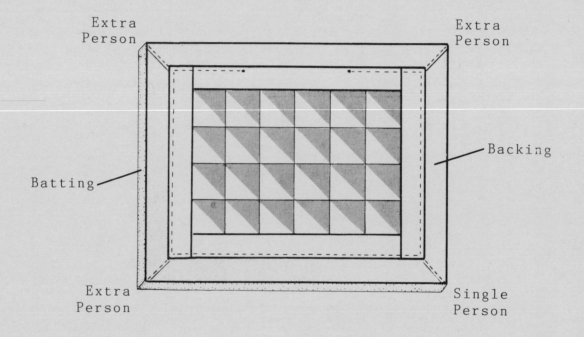

Turning the Quilt Top

This part of making your quilt is particularly exciting. One person can turn the quilt alone, but its so much fun to turn it into a 10 minute family or neighborhood event with three or four others.

Read this whole section before beginning.

If you are working with a group, station the people at the corners of the quilt. If working alone, start in one corner opposite the opening.

Roll the corners tightly to keep the batting in place. Roll the batting along the sides as tightly as you roll toward the opening.

If several people are helping, all should roll toward the opening. If only you are doing the rolling, use your knee to hold down one corner while stretching over to the other corners.

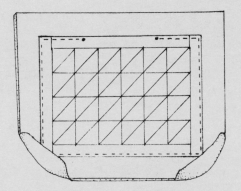

Roll all corners and sides towards the opening.

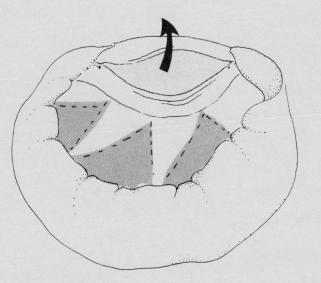

Open up the opening over this huge wad of fabric and batting and pop the quilt right side out through the hole.

Unroll it right side out very carefully with the layers together.

Lay the quilt out flat on the floor or on a very large table. Smooth and arrange the backing so that it comes around evenly on all sides.

Work out all wrinkles and bumps by stationing two people opposite each other around the quilt. Each grasp the edge and tug the quilt in opposite directions.

You can also relocate any batting by reaching inside the quilt through the opening with a yardstick. Hold the edges and shake the batting into place if necessary.

Whipstitch the opening shut.

Lay the quilt out on a large table. Smooth all layers.

Use a curved needle from a packaged assortment of needles. Tie with all six strands of embroidery floss, pearl cotton, wool yarn, or crochet thread.

Thread the needle with a long strand for multiple tying.

Plan where you want the stitches and dimension to be by pressing your fingers into the quilt at the various corners.

Working from the center out, take a stitch through all thicknesses in one corner of the block. **Do not cut the threads.**

Draw the needle over to the next corner to be tied and take a stitch. **Do not cut the threads.**

Take as many continuous stitches as the length of yarn will allow, stitching through all corners to be tied.

Cut all threads midway between the stitches.

Tie the yarn into a surgeon's square knot.

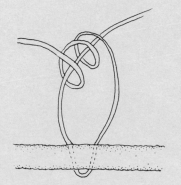 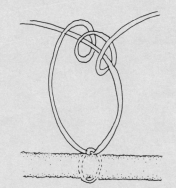

Right over left.
Wrap twice.
Pull tight.

Left over right.
Wrap twice.
Pull tight.

Clip the strands of yarn even to whatever length you wish.

Optional Tying Methods

Invisible Square Knot

For a knot that does not show on the right side of the quilt, place a pin at all the corners you wish to tie.

Flip the quilt over to the wrong side, and tie at all the pin marks.

Machine Tacking

Match the thread to the backing and Part B color. Put pins in at an angle at each corner you wish to tie.

Roll the quilt tightly from one long side toward the middle so the bulk will fit into the machine.

Work from the center down a row, taking several short stitches back and forth at each of the corners you wish to tack. Do not clip the threads each time, but allow them to trail from one tacking to the next.

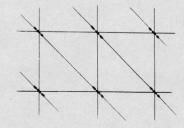

Unroll the quilt from the center out, tacking the corners in each of the long rows.

Work from the center out on the other side, repeating the same method.

Clip all threads.

Stitch in the Ditch (Optional)

For more dimensional borders, you may choose to "stitch in the ditch" around them rather than tie them.

Change your stitch length to 10 stitches per inch. Match your bobbin color of thread to your backing color.

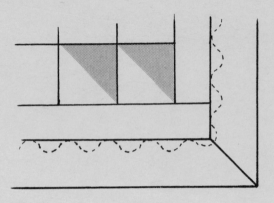

You may choose to use a decorative stitch known as the serpentine stitch for "stitching in the ditch." This stitch does not need to be as accurately "in the ditch" as a straight stitch to look attractive. Quite often, this is the stitch used by manufacturers for machine quilting.

Pin along the outside edge and the inside border. Place the needle in the depth of the seam and stitch.

You can avoid puckering on the back by:

Running your hand underneath to feel for puckers,
Grasping the quilt with your left hand above the sewing machine foot,
Grasping the quilt with your right hand 10" below the sewing machine foot,
Stretching between the two as you stitch.

To further avoid puckering on the back, you may choose to use an even feed foot or walking foot available for most sewing machines.

Acknowledgements

Front Cover: Quilt by Valerie Sullivan; Park Setting at Fluid Components, San Marcos, California.

Inside Back Cover: Color Selection and Pattern Layouts by Patricia Knoechel.

Back Cover: Color Selection and Layout by Patricia Knoechel; Quilt by Eleanor Burns; Park Setting at Fluid Components, San Marcos, California.

Slide Lecture on the Amish and their Quilts: Contact Deanna Hayes Nardozzo, 935 Oak Ridge Avenue, State College, Pennsylvania, 16801

Index

Book Order Information

If you do not have a fine quilting shop in your area, you may purchase these products from Eleanor Burns. Please write for a current price list of the supplies used.

Quilt in a Day

Make a beautiful log cabin quilt in 10-16 hours, using the speed-sew technique in the 91-page book. Concise, step-by-step directions with detailed illustrations are presented so even the beginner can find success. $10.95

Trio of Treasured Quilts

Three different patterns, Monkey Wrench, Ohio Star, and Bear's Paw are featured with quick, complete machine sewing methods. Make one block or a whole quilt following the detailed yardage charts, cutting or tearing charts, and assembly line sewing methods. The techniques are easy enough for a beginner or exciting enough for an experienced hand quilter. Other projects include pillows, aprons, tablecloths, and wallhangings. $11.95

The Sampler:
❖A Machine Sewn Quilt❖

Complete, detailed directions and illustrations show how to speed-sew a sampler quilt. The quilt is assembled using calicos, laces and trims for a nostalgic touch. All patterns are machine quilted on bonded batting for a soft, dimensional look. Instructions for smaller projects are also given. $11.95

Lover's Knot

The ease of assembly line sewing as in the log cabin blocks from Quilt in a Day is back! The Lover's Knot is quick to sew together in only 4 different colors. Additional features of the book include a sawtooth finished edge, and a simple-to sew dust ruffle. $7.95

Irish Chain

With two variations to choose from, the Irish Chain quilt is a favorite for beginners and advanced quilters alike. Strips are cut with a rotary cutter and assembly line sewn so you never have to work with tiny squares. Includes simple instructions and extensive illustrations. $7.95

May Basket

Make this delightful traditional pattern Amish in dark solid colors or Victorian in calicos with lace trim and a ruffle. The handle is easily made with a quick marking, sewing, and pressing technique. $7.95

COUNTRY CHRISTMAS SEWING

Ten festive decorations to sew in a twinkling are included in Eleanor's Country Christmas book. Complete full-sized patterns and step-by-step directions make the sewing a snap. $7.00

Bunnies & Blossoms

Contains full-sized patterns and detailed directions for 10 quick sewing projects, featuring sock Bunnies and their clothes. $7.00

Schoolhouse Wallhanging

A traditional pattern, the whole block is put together with the strip method, including the roof line! It's the perfect gift for the teacher or classroom. $5.00

DIAMOND LOG CABIN
TABLECLOTH OR TREESKIRT

Complement your country dining room decor with this 74" circular tablecloth! Twelve diamonds sew together easily with strip piecing and rotary cutting on the 60° angle. An added bonus is the large treeskirt! $5.00

Video Tapes

Take Eleanor home with you! Her enthusiasm is contagious! These titles are available in Beta or VHS: Log Cabin, Monkey Wrench, Ohio Star, Bear's Paw, Lover's Knot, Schoolhouse Wallhanging, Amish Quilt. Check on new titles available. Encourage your local public and video libraries to carry these tapes. **$39.95 each**

Radiant Star with Jan Donner, Creating with Color with Patricia Knoechel and Victorian Doll with Elinore Peace Bailey also available. **$29.95 each**

Patterns available:

Log Cabin Christmas Tree Wall Hanging
A delightful project to warm the Christmas spirit in your home, this 16 block pattern is assembly line sewn with 1 1/2" strips. Perfect for the holidays! **$4.00**

Easy Radiant Star Wall Hanging
Let this giant 40" x 40" multi-colored star brighten up your home! It's amazingly simple - thanks to rotary cutting with a ruler on the 45° line and strip piecing. **$4.00**

Country Patchwork Dress
This loosely flowing or belted country style dress with three different patchwork yokes is perfect for any season in a variety of fabrics. Full-sized patterns for women's sizes small through extra large and complete yardage charts! **$5.00**

Diamond Vest and Strip Vest
Detailed sewing instructions for a vest in six sizes are included. Described is a unique method of turning the lining so no hand-sewing is necessary. **$4.00**

Dresden Plate Placemats and Tea Cozy
Clear illustrations show how to speed cut and sew 16 wedges together quickly into the projects. **$3.50**

SHIPPING AND HANDLING RATES
for Books and Supplies ordered
from QUILT IN A DAY

$1.50 for First Item Ordered
  .50 for Each Item Ordered After
 3.00 for Video Tapes

FOREIGN ORDERS: Please add an
additional 20% in US Funds only.
California residents please add 6% sales tax.

Make check to:

Eleanor Burns
Quilt in a Day®
1955 Diamond Street, Unit
San Marcos, Ca. 92069